Sports and Activities
Let's Snowboard!

by Terri DeGezelle

Consulting Editor: Gail Saunders-Smith, PhD

Consultant: Kymm Ballard, MA
Physical Education, Athletics, and Sports Medicine Consultant
North Carolina Department of Public Instruction

Capstone press

Mankato, Minnesota

Pebble Plus is published by Capstone Press,
151 Good Counsel Drive, P.O. Box 669, Mankato, Minnesota 56002.
www.capstonepress.com

1 2 3 4 5 6 11 10 09 08 07 06

Library of Congress Cataloging-in-Publication Data
DeGezelle, Terri, 1955–
    Let's snowboard! / by Terri DeGezelle.
      p. cm. — (Pebble plus. Sports and activities)
    Includes bibliographical references and index.
    ISBN-13: 978-0-7368-5366-8 (hardcover)
    ISBN-10: 0-7368-5366-9 (hardcover)
    1. Snowboarding—Juvenile literature. I. Title. II. Series.
GV857.S57D44 2006
796.93'9—dc22   2005017939

Summary: Simple text and photographs present the skills, equipment, and safety concerns of snowboarding.

Editorial Credits
Heather Adamson, editor; Kia Adams, designer; Kelly Garvin, photo researcher

Photo Credits
All photos by Capstone Press/Karon Dubke except cover (background) by Shutterstock/JJJ

The author thanks Kyle Murray for sharing his knowledge of snowboarding.

Note to Parents and Teachers

The Sports and Activities set supports national physical education standards related
to recognizing movement forms and exhibiting a physically active lifestyle. This
book describes and illustrates snowboarding. The images support early readers in
understanding the text. The repetition of words and phrases helps early readers learn
new words. This book also introduces early readers to subject-specific vocabulary words,
which are defined in the Glossary section. Early readers may need assistance to read
some words and to use the Table of Contents, Glossary, Read More, Internet Sites, and
Index sections of the book.

Table of Contents

Snowboarding

Whoosh! Snowboarders slide
on frozen slopes.

They speed down snowy hills.

Snowboarders do tricks.

They jump.

They spin in the air.

Equipment

Snowboarders need boards
with bindings.
Bindings hold the board
to a snowboarder's boots.

binding

Snowboarders wear
warm clothes.
Hats and gloves keep skin
safe from the cold.

Goggles protect eyes
from sunlight, wind,
and spraying snow.

goggles

Boarding Safety

Snowboarders practice how
to fall safely.
They learn to tuck and roll.

Some snowboarders
wear helmets.
Helmets keep them safe in
crashes and falls.

Having Fun

Let's ride, speed,
and try not to fall!
Let's snowboard!

Glossary

bindings—straps and buckles that hold a snowboarder's boots to the board

goggles—tinted glasses that fit tightly around the eyes; goggles protect snowboarders' eyes from the sun's rays and falling snow.

helmet—a hard hat that protects the head during sports activities

practice—to do something over and over again to try to learn to do it better

protect—to guard or to keep safe from injury

slope—a section of ground with a steep angle; a side of a hill.

Read More

Doeden, Matt. *Snowboarding.* To the Extreme. Mankato, Minn.: Capstone Press, 2005.

Eckart, Edana. *I Can Snowboard.* Sports. New York: Children's Press, 2003.

Woods, Bob. *Snowboarding.* Kids' Guides. Chanhassen, Minn.: Child's World, 2005.

Internet Sites

FactHound offers a safe, fun way to find Internet sites related to this book. All of the sites on FactHound have been researched by our staff.

Here's how:

1. Visit *www.facthound.com*

2. Type in this special code **0736853669** for age-appropriate sites. Or enter a search word related to this book for a more general search.

3. Click on the **Fetch It** button.

FactHound will fetch the best sites for you!

Index

Word Count: 90
Grade: 1
Early-Intervention Level: 13